PICKLES &
PRESERVES

PICKLES & PRESERVES

Easy recipes for delicious
home-made pickles
& preserves

This edition published in 2013
LOVE FOOD is an imprint of Parragon Books Ltd

Parragon
Chartist House
15–17 Trim Street
Bath, BA1 1HA, UK

Copyright © Parragon Books Ltd 2012

LOVE FOOD and the accompanying heart device is a registered trade mark of Parragon Books Ltd
in Australia, the UK, USA, India and the EU.

www.parragon.com/lovefood

ISBN: 978-1-4454-9961-1

Printed in China

Cover and internal design by Itonic Design
New recipes by Linda Doeser
New photography by Clive Streeter
New home economy by Teresa Goldfinch and Sally Streeter

Notes for the Reader
This book uses both metric and imperial measurements. Follow the same units of measurement throughout;
do not mix metric and imperial. All spoon measurements are level: teaspoons are assumed to be 5 ml,
and tablespoons are assumed to be 15 ml. Unless otherwise stated, milk is assumed to be full fat, eggs
and individual vegetables are medium, and pepper is freshly ground black pepper. Unless otherwise
stated, all root vegetables should be washed and peeled prior to using.

Garnishes, decorations and serving suggestions are all optional and not necessarily included in the recipe
ingredients or method.

The times given are an approximate guide only. Preparation times differ according to the techniques
used by different people and the cooking times may also vary from those given. Optional ingredients,
variations or serving suggestions have not been included in the time calculations.

Recipes using raw or very lightly cooked eggs should be avoided by infants, the elderly, pregnant women,
convalescents and anyone suffering from an illness. Pregnant and breastfeeding women are advised to
avoid eating peanuts and peanut products. Sufferers from nut allergies should be aware that some of the
ready-made ingredients used in the recipes in this book may contain nuts. Always check the packaging
before use.

Picture acknowledgements
The publisher would like to thank the following for permission to reproduce copyright images:
Illustrations (throughout) Cooking Goods © iStockPhoto.com; Spotty background (throughout) White d
yellow © iStockPhoto.com; Gingham background (throughout) Checked cloth pattern © iStockPhoto

CONTENTS

GETTING STARTED

Savour seasonal specialities all year round with your own home-made jams, jellies, marmalades, fruit curds, butters and cheeses. With just basic kitchen equipment and a little time, you can produce preserves that are delicious and inexpensive. The introduction that follows explains the essentials for preserving produce at home.

There are a whole host of traditional preserves that simply aren't available from the supermarket – sweet and savoury alike – which make a delicious addition to your store cupboard. Jams and conserves are perhaps the most popular preserves (made from a mixture of fruits and sugar), but there are also jellies (which are strained before cooling), marmalades (made largely from citrus fruits), curds (which contain eggs and sugar), butters and fruit cheeses (made from concentrated fruit purée) and savoury chutneys, pickles and relishes.

SETTING POINTS

One term which crops up in almost all of the following recipes is 'setting point' – this is the moment during cooking when the preserve has been boiling long enough to solidify to a spreading consistency when cold. The easiest way to check for setting point when making jam is to use a sugar thermometer; when the temperature reaches 110°C/225°F, it should be removed from the heat and potted. Make sure that the thermometer does not touch the base or sides of the pan as this would affect the reading.

If you don't own a sugar thermometer, there are a variety of less technical but equally effective methods that can be used for each type of preserve. To test jams, conserves, jellies and marmalades, place a few small saucers into the freezer. When you think the preserve is reaching setting point (using the time listed in the recipe as a guide), remove the pan from the heat and put a teaspoonful of the preserve onto one of the chilled saucers. When cooled, gently push the surface with the tip of your finger. If it wrinkles, the preserve has reached setting point. If the surface doesn't wrinkle, return the pan to the heat for a few minutes more, then retest.

You can test fruit butter for setting point by putting a teaspoonful on a saucer at room temperature; if no liquid runs out, it is ready. Test fruit cheese by drawing a wooden spoon across the base of the preserving pan; if it leaves a clean line, setting point has been reached. Testing chutney is similar – make a channel across the surface with a wooden spoon; if the channel remains for a few seconds without flooding with vinegar, the chutney is ready for potting. Curd is ready when the mixture is thick enough to coat the back of a wooden spoon.

Whatever you're making, remember that practice makes perfect – who cares if your jam ends up a little runny, or sets a little too solid – it's sure to taste absolutely delicious!

FRUIT & VEG

There's no denying the simple pleasure of sweet, lightly spiced jam on freshly baked, buttered bread, but for centuries the process of preserving fruits and vegetables was quite simply the best way of prolonging the life of seasonal food that was abundant in summer and autumn, to be eaten in the leaner winter months.

Of course, now that fresh produce is transported across the world every day and every kitchen has a freezer, such techniques are no longer essential for ensuring a varied supply of fruit and vegetables throughout the colder months. Nevertheless, there is something incredibly satisfying about preserving a particular harvest, and with many of us returning to a grow-your-own ethos, it can be a practical way of making good use of gluts of home-grown crops. A bumper crop of tomatoes or apples can only be transformed into so many dishes before you're craving an alternative but, with a little sugar, some spice and herbs, you can make tasty preserves to enjoy all year round.

PECTIN & FRUIT ACID

Always use fruit and vegetables in top condition – poor quality ingredients will only result in second-rate preserves. Slightly under-ripe fruit is best for jams, jellies, fruit butters and cheeses as it contains more fruit acid and pectin (a natural setting agent) than very ripe fruit. Some fruits don't naturally contain high levels of pectin, so either liquid or powdered pectin (available from supermarkets) needs to be added during the jam-making process. Alternatively, the fruit can be combined with one containing high levels of pectin – this balancing of pectin levels has resulted in a number of favoured flavour combinations, such as apple and blackberry – the first fruit being high in pectin and the second low.

Levels of fruit acid are also important. This naturally occurring acid is released when the fruit is boiled with sugar and in the process all three components – sugar, pectin and fruit acid – combine, and eventually this combination reaches setting point. If fruits are low in fruit acids, the deficiency is usually rectified by adding lemon juice, and this will be listed in the recipe, if necessary.

PREPARATION

Avoid washing fruits and vegetables in lots of water as this is likely to dilute both the pectin and fruit acid. If you must wash them, pat dry with kitchen paper before using, but, ideally, simply wipe with damp kitchen paper. Bear in mind that boiling the fruit or vegetables will, to all intents and purposes, sterilize them.

Some recipes call for the stones from within fruits – these are a natural aid to the setting process. Where necessary, reserve the stones, prepare as advised in the recipe and then tie in a square of muslin. Add to the boiling mixture when instructed in the method text.

EQUIPMENT

For most preserves, it's perfectly possible simply to use everyday kitchen utensils, but for some of the slightly more refined recipes, such as those for jellies, a little extra kit is necessary for optimum results. Most items can be bought from specialist kitchen shops, or online, at a relatively small cost.

• A heavy-based preserving pan or saucepan is essential. Ideally, your pan should have a pouring lip with an ear-shaped handle on the opposite side, as well as a longer, central handle for lifting the pan. A graded scale marked on the inside of the pan is particularly useful when making jelly, fruit butters and cheeses, as the quantity of sugar depends on the quantity of juice or purée. A 9-litre/15¾-pint pan is a good size for most home cooks.

• A jelly strainer consists of a plastic stand fitted with a muslin bag for straining the juice from cooked fruit for making jelly. The bag can be removed for emptying and washing. There is room underneath the stand for a bowl, to collect the juice. Alternatively, you can strain preserves through a fine-mesh sieve (non-metallic for acidic jellies) into a clean, dry bowl.

• Small muslin squares are available from kitchen suppliers. These are useful for wrapping pickling spices, herbs and fruit stones or pips – for easy removal before cooling. You could also use ordinary gauze, available from pharmacies (provided it has not been impregnated with antiseptic!).

• Jars and lids are, of course, essential for potting preserves. You can buy them from kitchen suppliers and on the internet, or simply save and wash commercial jars. The lids for recipes containing vinegar or substantial quantities of lemon, lime or orange juice should be plastic coated to avoid corrosion. Proper preserving jars with an airtight rubber seal are more expensive but will last a lifetime and are particularly good for storing pickles.

• A jam funnel is inexpensive but very useful as it helps to prevent sticky drips down the outside of jars when they are being filled.

• Waxed discs are available from kitchen shops, stationers and on the internet. These little discs of paper covered with a thin layer of wax are placed on top of the freshly potted preserve, wax-side down, while it is still hot, to form a seal. The jars may then be covered with lids. Jams, jellies, marmalades, fruit butters and cheeses may also be covered with cellophane covers held in place with elastic bands but these are not suitable for pickles, relishes, chutneys or any other preserves containing vinegar.

• You should always label jars with their contents and the date – use the self-adhesive labels within this book, but remember to stick on once completely cold, otherwise they will not adhere properly.

STORAGE

The clue is in the name – preserves will keep for a long time – up to a year is not uncommon. To ensure that they retain the best quality and flavour there are some rules which should be followed, both when potting and storing, and these differ for each of the different preserves, according to its ingredients.

Always store preserves (apart from curds and fresh chutneys or relishes) in a cool, dark, dry place, as light and heat will adversely affect the flavour, while damp or a steamy room can cause mould to grow on the surface of jam. If mould does form on the surface of the preserve, scoop it off with a teaspoon and then remove the top 2 cm/¾ inch of jam. Then before re-sealing, dip a waxed disc in a strong alcoholic spirit such as brandy or vodka (to sterilize), put it on the surface of the jam and re-cover the jar.

CURDS

Curds are not, strictly speaking, preserves as they contain eggs. Once cooled and covered, they should be stored in the refrigerator and eaten within two to three weeks. As a result, you will notice that these recipes make a smaller quantity than the other preserves.

CHUTNEY

While jams, marmalades and jellies can be eaten more or less immediately, chutneys often need to be left to mature. If eaten immediately, they can taste vinegary, as it takes time for the flavours to mellow. They must be stored for at least four weeks and, ideally, should be stored for up to three months, before consuming. This is also true of many pickles.

For this reason, writing the date on which you sealed the jars and labelling them correctly, is essential!

RELISHES

Some fresh chutneys and relishes are intended for immediate consumption – where this is the case, you will find that the recipe states as much. If you want to store these particular recipes for consumption at a later date, pack into a freezer-proof container and freeze for up to one month.

To be on the safe side, it is best to store all preserves in the refrigerator once they have been opened and use within the time listed in each of the recipes. Trust your common sense – if you open a jar and it doesn't look or smell right, don't eat it!

HEALTH & SAFETY

It's important that you adhere to a number of safety measures when potting pickles and preserves, as any bacteria that is unwittingly sealed in with the produce can multiply whilst in storage. There are simple steps to sterilize the necessary equipment that will help to keep you, and your kitchen produce, safe.

It goes without saying that jam-making involves lots of hot liquids, so one of the most important things to be aware of is your own safety in the kitchen! Always use a preserving pan that is large enough to 'contain' splutters from the cooking liquid, and use a ladle to decant the finished preserve from the pan to the jars (never try to lift a heavy pan). Before starting, clear your work space and lay out any necessary equipment or ingredients within easy reach for when the process begins.

STERILIZING JARS

Always wash jars and lids, even new ones, in hot soapy water and rinse well before using. Stand the uncovered jars, right way up, on a baking sheet and put them into a preheated oven, 180°C/350°F/Gas Mark 4, for at least 5 minutes. This makes sure that they are dry, sterilizes them and prevents the glass from cracking when the hot preserve is poured in. Generally you will find that the recipes call for a cooling period of 10–15 minutes before transferring to jars – this is the perfect window of time to heat the jars in the oven.

Alternatively, you can use a hot wash cycle on your dishwasher to sterilize jars, timing the washing and drying cycle to finish just before you need hot jars to fill.

SKIMMING & POTTING

When jams and jellies are boiling, scum often rises to the surface. This is a natural part of the process and is not harmful. Skim off this scum once you have removed the pan from the heat. If any remains, stir in a knob of butter and this will disperse it.

Even if you use a jam funnel to fill the jars, you can still end up with splashes on the outsides. Wipe these off immediately with a cloth wrung out in hot water.

Fill the jars as full as possible while the jam is hot and seal immediately with a waxed disc. This should be placed wax-side down, and then smoothed across the surface to remove any pockets of air. Seal with a lid while hot, then leave to cool before labelling. Always label preserves with the date of making, and leave space to include the date of opening, too.

JAMS & CONSERVES

STRAWBERRY JAM

MAKES:
1.5 kg/
3 lb 5 oz

PREP TIME:
5–10 minutes,
plus cooling

COOKING TIME:
30–40 minutes

1.5 kg/3 lb 5 oz whole strawberries, hulled and rinsed

juice of 2 lemons

1.5 kg/3 lb 5 oz jam sugar

1 tsp butter

1. Place the strawberries in a preserving pan with the lemon juice, then simmer over a gentle heat for 15–20 minutes, stirring occasionally, until the fruit is soft.

2. Add the sugar and heat, stirring occasionally, until the sugar has completely dissolved. Add the butter, then bring to the boil and boil rapidly for 10–20 minutes, or until setting point is reached.

3. Remove from the heat and leave to cool for 8–10 minutes, then ladle into sterilized jars and cover the tops with waxed discs. Seal with lids while hot, then leave to cool before labelling. Store in a cool, dark place. Once opened, store in the refrigerator.

PEACH & PASSION FRUIT JAM

MAKES:
2.5 kg/
5 lb 8 oz

PREP TIME:
10 minutes,
plus cooling

COOKING TIME:
40–45 minutes

900 g/2 lb peaches, rinsed

4 ripe passion fruits

150 ml/5 fl oz freshly squeezed lemon juice

900 g/2 lb preserving sugar

1. Make a small cross at the stalk end of each peach and place in a large bowl. Cover with boiling water and leave to stand for 2–3 minutes. Drain and leave to cool. When cool enough to handle, peel off the skins. Cut the peaches in half and discard the stones. Place the fruit in a preserving pan. Cut the passion fruit in half, scoop out the pulp and seeds and add to the peaches.

2. Add the lemon juice and sugar, place over a gentle heat and simmer for 30 minutes, or until the fruit is soft. Bring to the boil and boil rapidly for 15 minutes, or until setting point is reached.

3. Remove from the heat and leave to cool for 10–15 minutes, then ladle into sterilized jars and cover the tops with waxed discs. Seal with lids while hot, then leave to cool before labelling. Store in a cool, dark place. Once opened, store in the refrigerator.

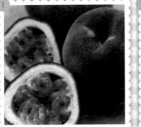

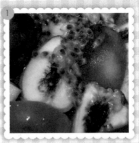

PLUM JAM

MAKES:
2.25 kg/
5 lb

PREP TIME:
10 minutes,
plus cooling

COOKING TIME:
50–55 minutes

1.5 kg/3 lb 5 oz plums, rinsed

450 ml/16 fl oz water

1.5 kg/3 lb 5 oz preserving sugar

1 tsp butter

1. Remove the stalks from the plums, then cut in half and remove the stones. Crack a few of the stones open, remove the kernels and tie them in a piece of muslin.

2. Place the plums, reserved kernels and water in a preserving pan, bring to the boil, then reduce the heat and simmer for 40 minutes, or until soft. Add the sugar and heat gently, stirring frequently, until the sugar has completely dissolved, then add the butter. Bring to the boil and boil rapidly for 10–15 minutes, or until setting point is reached.

3. Remove from the heat and leave to cool for 8–10 minutes, then remove the kernels and ladle into sterilized jars and cover the tops with waxed discs. Seal with lids while hot, then leave to cool before labelling. Store in a cool, dark place. Once opened, store in the refrigerator.

Cook's tip: Add spices for a fruity kick! Try boiling them up with the plums, then remove before adding the sugar – 6 lightly cracked cardamom pods or a couple of lightly bruised lemon grass stalks give a warming zing to plum jam.

APRICOT JAM

MAKES:
2.7 kg/
6 lb

PREP TIME:
10–15 minutes,
plus cooling

COOKING TIME:
35–40 minutes

1.8 kg/4 lb apricots

150 ml/5 fl oz freshly squeezed lemon juice

1.8 kg/4 lb jam sugar

55 g/2 oz dried cranberries

25 g/1 oz flaked almonds

1. Rinse and chop the apricots, removing the central stones and setting aside. Place in a heavy-based saucepan, add the lemon juice, and cook over a medium heat for 20–25 minutes, or until soft. Remove from the heat and pour into a preserving pan.

2. Using a nut cracker, open a few of the apricot stones and remove and reserve the kernels within. Blanch the apricot kernels in boiling water, then tie in a little muslin and add to the pan with the fruit.

3. Add the sugar and cook gently, stirring occasionally, until the sugar has completely dissolved. Stir in the cranberries, bring to the boil and boil for 15 minutes, or until setting point is reached. Remove from the heat and leave to cool for 5 minutes. Remove the kernels and stir in the flaked almonds.

4. Ladle into warmed sterilized jars and cover the tops with waxed discs. Seal with lids while hot, then leave to cool before labelling. Store in a cool, dark place. Once opened, store in the refrigerator.

Cook's tip: If you prefer jam without the bits, simply peel the apricots before cooking, and omit the cranberries and almonds.

RHUBARB & ELDERFLOWER JAM

 MAKES:
1.8 kg/
4 lb

 PREP TIME:
40 minutes,
plus standing
and cooling

 COOKING TIME:
1 hour

10 elderflower tea bags

1.5 kg/3 lb 5 oz rhubarb, trimmed and cut into 2.5-cm/1-inch lengths

1.5 kg/3 lb 5 oz granulated sugar

juice of 1 lemon

1. Put half the elderflower tea bags on the bottom of a large non-metallic bowl. Add half the rhubarb and sprinkle with half the sugar, then repeat the layers with the remaining tea bags, rhubarb and sugar. Cover with clingfilm and shake gently to mix the ingredients. Leave to stand for 12 hours.

2. Uncover the bowl and stir the rhubarb mixture, then re-cover the bowl and leave to stand for a further 12 hours.

3. Uncover the bowl and tip the mixture into a preserving pan or large saucepan. Set over a medium heat and bring to simmering point, stirring constantly to make sure that all the sugar has dissolved. Remove the pan from the heat and return the rhubarb mixture to the bowl. Re-cover with clingfilm and leave to stand for another 12 hours.

4. Uncover the bowl and tip the mixture into a preserving pan or large saucepan. Remove and discard the tea bags. Stir in the lemon juice and bring to a boil over a high heat, then reduce the heat and simmer for about 45 minutes, or until setting point is reached.

5. Remove the pan from the heat and leave to cool for 15 minutes, then ladle into sterilized jars and cover the tops with waxed discs. Seal with lids while hot, then leave to cool before labelling. Store in a cool, dark place. Once opened, store in the refrigerator.

MARROW & GINGER CONSERVE

MAKES:
1.8 kg/4 lb

PREP TIME:
30–40 minutes,
plus standing
and cooling

COOKING TIME:
40–50 minutes

1.8 kg/4 lb marrow, peeled, deseeded and cut into 2.5-cm/1-inch cubes

juice and thinly pared rind of 4 lemons

½ cinnamon stick

4-cm/1½-inch piece fresh ginger

1.3 kg/3 lb granulated sugar

115 g/4 oz crystallized ginger, chopped .

1. Put the marrow into a steamer, set it over a pan of boiling water, cover and steam for 25 minutes, until tender. Remove from the heat and tip into a large bowl.

2. Add the lemon juice to the bowl. Tie the lemon rind, cinnamon stick and fresh ginger in a piece of muslin and add to the bowl, then stir in the sugar. Cover the bowl with clingfilm and leave to stand for 24 hours.

3. Tip the mixture into a preserving pan or other large saucepan and heat gently, stirring constantly, until the sugar has completely dissolved. Increase the heat to medium and bring to the boil, then boil for 20–30 minutes, or until setting point is reached.

4. Remove from the heat. Remove and discard the spices and skim off any scum from the surface. Stir in the crystallized ginger and leave to cool for 10–15 minutes. Ladle into sterilized jars and cover the tops with waxed discs. Seal with lids while hot, then leave to cool before labelling. Store in a cool, dark place. Once opened, store in the refrigerator.

CHERRY BRANDY JAM

MAKES:
2.25 kg/
5 lb

PREP TIME:
10 minutes,
plus cooling

COOKING TIME:
25–30 minutes

1.8 kg/4 lb dark cherries, such as Morello, rinsed and stoned

125 ml/4 fl oz freshly squeezed lemon juice

1.25 kg/2 lb 12 oz granulated sugar

1 tsp butter

4 tbsp brandy

225 ml/8 fl oz liquid pectin

1. Rinse and stone the cherries, then roughly chop and place in a large preserving pan with the lemon juice. Place the pan over a gentle heat, cover and simmer gently for 20 minutes, or until the cherries are soft.

2. Add the sugar and heat, stirring frequently, until the sugar has completely dissolved. Add the butter and brandy, bring to the boil and boil rapidly for 3 minutes. Remove from the heat and stir in the pectin.

3. Leave to cool for 10 minutes then ladle into sterilized jars and cover the tops with waxed discs. Seal with lids while hot, then leave to cool before labelling. Store in a cool, dark place. Once opened, store in the refrigerator.

Cook's tip: Cherries are the perfect partner for strong liqueurs, so if brandy's not your favourite tipple, try the same quantity of kirsch, Cointreau or whisky instead!

PEAR CONSERVE

MAKES:
900 g/2 lb

PREP TIME:
40 minutes,
plus cooling

COOKING TIME:
55 minutes–
1 hour

150 ml/5 fl oz pear cider or
sweet apple cider

1 kg/2 lb 4 oz pears,
finely chopped

675 g/1lb 8 oz granulated
sugar

juice of 2 lemons

1. Pour the cider into a large saucepan, bring to the boil and add the pears. Reduce the heat, cover and simmer for 25–30 minutes, until very tender.

2. Remove the pan from the heat and transfer the mixture to a blender or food processor and process until puréed. Rub the purée through a sieve into a clean pan.

3. Set the pan over a low heat, add the sugar and stir constantly until it has completely dissolved. Stir in the lemon juice, increase the heat and bring to the boil. Boil, stirring constantly, for 30 minutes, or until setting point is reached.

4. Remove from the heat and leave to cool for 5–10 minutes, then ladle into sterilized jars and cover with waxed discs. Seal with lids while hot, then leave to cool before labelling. Store in a cool, dark place. Once opened, store in the refrigerator.

GOOSEBERRY CONSERVE

MAKES:
1.3 kg/3 lb

PREP TIME:
10 minutes,
plus cooling

COOKING TIME:
40–45 minutes

1.25 kg/2 lb 12 oz gooseberries

140 g/5 oz raisins

1½ oranges peeled, deseeded and chopped

800 g/1 lb 12 oz granulated sugar

1. Trim the tails of the gooseberries, then place them in a preserving pan with the raisins, oranges and sugar. Bring to the boil over a low heat, stirring constantly until the juices run and the sugar has dissolved.

2. Increase the heat and boil, stirring occasionally, for about 30 minutes, or until setting point is reached.

3. Remove from the heat and leave to cool for 8–10 minutes, then ladle into sterilized jars and cover the tops with waxed discs. Seal with lids while hot, then leave to cool before labelling. Store in a cool, dark place. Once opened, store in the refrigerator.

Cook's tip: Gooseberries (especially when picked early in the season) can be incredibly tart, but the resulting conserve is delicious when contrasted with a super-sweet accompaniment, like ice cream. If you prefer sweeter jam for your toast, pick very ripe gooseberries, or use canned or frozen instead.

SWEET CHILLI JAM

MAKES:
1.3 kg/3 lb

PREP TIME:
30 minutes,
plus cooling

COOKING TIME:
55 minutes–
1 hour

10–12 fresh red chillies,
very finely chopped

8 red peppers, deseeded and
very finely chopped

5-cm/2-inch piece fresh
ginger, very finely chopped

10 garlic cloves, very finely
chopped

400 g/14 oz canned cherry
tomatoes

250 ml/9 fl oz red wine vinegar

750 g/1 lb 10 oz granulated
sugar

1. Put all the ingredients into a preserving pan or large saucepan. Set over a low heat and stir until the sugar has dissolved, then increase the heat and bring to the boil.

2. Reduce the heat and simmer, stirring occasionally, for about 45 minutes, until reduced. Increase the heat and continue to cook, stirring frequently, for a further 10–15 minutes, or until thickened.

3. Remove from the heat and leave to cool for 5–10 minutes, then ladle into sterilized jars and cover the tops with waxed discs. Seal with non-metallic lids while hot, then leave to cool before labelling. Store in a cool, dark place. Once opened, store in the refrigerator.

TOMATO & HERB CONSERVE

MAKES:
250 ml/8 fl oz

PREP TIME:
20 minutes,
plus cooling

COOKING TIME:
25 minutes

1 tbsp olive oil

550 g/1 lb 4 oz ripe tomatoes,
peeled and chopped

2 garlic cloves, finely chopped

1 tbsp chopped flat-leaf
parsley

2 tbsp chopped basil

1 tbsp chopped tarragon

1 tbsp red wine vinegar

pepper

1. Heat the oil in a frying pan, add the tomatoes, garlic and herbs and cook over a medium heat, shaking the pan occasionally, for 15 minutes.

2. Gently stir in the vinegar and season to taste with pepper. Continue to cook, shaking the pan occasionally, for a further 10 minutes, or until thickened.

3. Remove from the heat and leave to cool for 10–15 minutes. Serve immediately or pack into a non-metallic airtight container and store in the refrigerator for up to 1 week. Alternatively, freeze for up to 1 month.

TOMATO & CHILLI JAM

 MAKES:
700 g/
1 lb 9 oz

 PREP TIME:
30 minutes,
plus standing
and cooling

 COOKING TIME:
1¼–1¾ hours

1 kg/2 lb 4 oz tomatoes,
peeled and chopped

500 g/1 lb 2 oz granulated
sugar

8 fresh red chillies, deseeded
and chopped

3 tbsp lemon juice

5 tbsp white wine vinegar

2 tsp salt

1. Put the tomatoes into a non-metallic bowl and stir in the sugar. Cover the bowl with clingfilm and leave to stand for 8 hours, or overnight.

2. Transfer the tomato mixture to a preserving pan and add all the remaining ingredients. Bring to the boil over a medium heat, stirring until the sugar has completely dissolved.

3. Reduce the heat and simmer, stirring occasionally, for 1–1½ hours, or until thickened. Remove from the heat and leave to cool for 8–10 minutes, then ladle into sterilized jars and cover the tops with waxed discs. Seal with non-metallic lids while hot, then leave to cool before labelling. Store in a cool, dark place. Once opened, store in the refrigerator.

ROAST GARLIC, ONION &
BALSAMIC JAM

MAKES:
450 g/1 lb

PREP TIME:
15 minutes,
plus cooling

COOKING TIME:
1½–1¾ hours

2 garlic bulbs, central stems removed

2 bay leaves

2–3 thyme sprigs

1 tbsp lemon juice

4 tbsp olive oil

850 g/1 lb 14 oz sweet onions, halved and thickly sliced

2 tbsp granulated sugar

2 tbsp soft brown sugar

4 tbsp water

4 tbsp balsamic vinegar

salt and pepper

1. Preheat the oven to 200°C/400°F/Gas Mark 6. Place the garlic bulbs in a small ovenproof dish. Wrap a bay leaf around each bulb, season with salt and pepper and cover with the thyme sprigs. Sprinkle with the lemon juice, drizzle with half the olive oil and cover with foil. Roast the garlic for 10 minutes, then remove from the oven, uncover and baste. Reduce the oven temperature to 160°C/325°F/Gas Mark 3. Re-cover the garlic, return it to the oven and roast for a further 40 minutes, or until soft.

2. Meanwhile, heat the remaining oil in a large frying pan, add the onions and cook over a medium heat, stirring occasionally, for 15 minutes. Stir in both types of sugar, cover the pan and continue to cook, for 25–30 minutes, until golden.

3. Remove the garlic from the oven and leave to cool. Squeeze out the cloves on to a plate and set aside.

4. Stir the water into the onions, re-cover the pan and cook, stirring occasionally, for a further 25–30 minutes, until a deep brown colour. Stir in the vinegar and garlic and cook, stirring and mashing the garlic occasionally, for 10–15 minutes, or until all the liquid has been absorbed.

5. Remove from the heat and leave to cool for 10–15 minutes, then ladle into a sterilized jar. Seal with a non-metallic lid while hot, then leave to cool before labelling. Store in a cool, dark place. Once opened, store in the refrigerator.

JELLIES & MARMALADES

CRANBERRY JELLY

MAKES:
1 kg/
2 lb 4 oz

PREP TIME:
5–10 minutes,
plus straining
and cooling

COOKING TIME:
1–1¼ hours

900 g/2 lb fresh cranberries, washed

2 large oranges (preferably unwaxed), scrubbed and cut into wedges

1 lemon (preferably unwaxed), scrubbed and cut into wedges

850 ml/1½ pints water

about 450 g/1 lb preserving sugar (see method)

1. Place the cranberries, oranges and lemon in a preserving pan. Add the water, bring to the boil, then reduce the heat and simmer for 45 minutes, or until the cranberries are soft. Remove the pan from the heat and pour the mixture into a jelly strainer set over a bowl.

2. Once all the juice has been extracted, measure and return to the rinsed-out preserving pan. Add the sugar, allowing 450 g/1 lb of sugar for every 600 ml/ 1 pint of juice. Heat gently, stirring frequently, until the sugar has completely dissolved.

3. Bring to the boil and boil rapidly for 15 minutes, or until setting point is reached. Remove from the heat and leave to cool for 5–10 minutes, then ladle into sterilized jars and cover the tops with waxed discs. Seal with non-metallic lids while hot, then leave to cool before labelling. Store in a cool, dark place. Once opened, store in the refrigerator.

Cook's tip: Cranberry jelly is delicious with poultry – add 2–3 whole cloves when simmering the fruits, for a spicy flavour that's the perfect accompaniment to your Sunday roast.

CINNAMON APPLE JELLY

MAKES:
675 g/
1 lb 8 oz

PREP TIME:
1 hour,
plus straining
and cooling

COOKING TIME:
1–1¼ hours

1.8 kg/4 lb tart apples, cored and cut into eighths

2 cinnamon sticks

1.2 litres/2 pints water

about 1.8 kg/4 lb granulated sugar (see method)

1. Put the apples and cinnamon sticks into a preserving pan or large saucepan, pour in the water and bring to the boil over a high heat. Reduce the heat to medium and simmer, stirring occasionally, for 40–50 minutes, until the apples are soft.

2. Remove the pan from the heat and pour the apples and liquid into a jelly strainer set over a bowl. Leave to drain overnight without squeezing the bag.

3. Measure the final quantity of juice and pour it into a preserving pan. Add 450 g/1 lb sugar for every 600 ml/1 pint juice. Set the pan over a low heat and stir constantly until the sugar has dissolved. Increase the heat to high and bring to the boil. Boil for 15–25 minutes, or until setting point is reached.

4. Remove from the heat and skim off any scum from the surface then ladle into sterilized jars and cover the tops with waxed discs. Seal with non-metallic lids while hot, then leave to cool before labelling. Store in a cool dark place. Once opened, store in the refrigerator.

RHUBARB & STRAWBERRY JELLY

MAKES:
1.75 kg/
3 lb 14 oz

PREP TIME:
10–15 minutes,
plus straining
and cooling

COOKING TIME:
1¼–1½ hours

675 g/1 lb 8 oz rhubarb,
trimmed, washed and cut into
2.5-cm/1-inch lengths

1.2 litres/2 pints water

900 g/2 lb strawberries,
hulled and rinsed

5-cm/2-inch piece fresh
ginger, peeled and chopped

about 900 g/2 lb preserving
sugar (see method)

1. Place the rhubarb in a preserving pan with the water, strawberries and ginger and simmer over a gentle heat for 1 hour, or until the fruits are soft.

2. Strain the mixture through a jelly bag. Once all the juice has been extracted, measure and return to the rinsed-out preserving pan. Add the sugar, allowing 450 g/1 lb of sugar for every 600 ml/1 pint of juice. Heat gently, stirring frequently, until the sugar has completely dissolved, then bring to the boil and boil rapidly for 10–15 minutes, or until setting point is reached.

3. Remove from the heat and leave to cool for 5–10 minutes, then ladle into sterilized jars and cover the tops with waxed discs. Seal with non-metallic lids while hot, then leave to cool before labelling. Store in a cool, dark place. Once opened, store in the refrigerator.

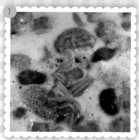

RED PEPPER & CHILLI JELLY

MAKES:
675 g/
1 lb 8 oz

PREP TIME:
15–20 minutes
plus straining
and cooling

COOKING TIME:
1¼–1½ hours

3 serrano red chillies,
or according to taste

8 red peppers, deseeded and
roughly chopped

2 Bramley apples, washed and
roughly chopped

150 ml/5 fl oz white wine
vinegar

1.4 litres/2½ pints water

1 tbsp coriander seeds,
lightly crushed

5-cm/2-inch piece fresh
ginger, peeled and grated

about 900 g/2 lb preserving
sugar (see method)

225 ml/8 fl oz liquid pectin

1. Cut each of the chillies in half, discard the seeds
and finely chop the flesh. Place 2 of the chillies, the
peppers and apples in a preserving pan with the
vinegar, water, coriander seeds and ginger. Bring to the
boil, then reduce the heat and simmer for 1 hour, or
until the peppers are tender. Strain through a jelly bag.

2. Once all the liquid has been extracted, measure
and return to the rinsed-out preserving pan. Add the
sugar, allowing 450 g/1 lb of sugar for every 600 ml/
1 pint of pepper juice. Heat gently, stirring frequently,
until the sugar has completely dissolved, then bring to
the boil and boil rapidly for 3 minutes, or until setting
point is reached.

3. Remove from the heat and leave to cool for
5 minutes. Stir in the pectin and the remaining
chopped chilli, then ladle into sterilized jars and
cover the tops with waxed discs. Seal with non-metallic
lids while hot, then leave to cool before labelling.
Store in a cool, dark place. Once opened, store in
the refrigerator.

CRAB APPLE JELLY

MAKES:
1.5 kg/
3 lb 5 oz

PREP TIME:
1¼ hours,
plus straining
and cooling

COOKING TIME:
1½–1¾ hours

1.8 kg/4 lb crab apples, stalks removed, cut into quarters

thinly pared rind of 2 lemons

about 1.6 kg/3 lb 8 oz granulated sugar (see method)

1. Put the crab apples into a large preserving pan, pour in enough water to cover and add the lemon rind. Bring to the boil over a high heat, then reduce the heat to medium and simmer, stirring occasionally, for 1 hour, until the apples are soft.

2. Remove the pan from the heat and pour the apples and liquid into a jelly strainer set over a bowl. Leave to drain overnight without squeezing the bag.

3. Measure the final quantity of juice and pour it into a preserving pan. Add 450 g/1 lb sugar for every 600 ml/1 pint juice. Set the pan over a low heat and stir constantly, until the sugar has dissolved. Increase the heat to high and bring to the boil. Boil for 15–25 minutes, or until setting point is reached.

4. Remove from the heat and leave to cool for 8–10 minutes, then ladle into sterilized jars and cover with waxed discs. Seal with non-metallic lids while hot, then leave to cool before labelling. Store in a cool, dark place. Once opened, store in the refrigerator.

CHUNKY TOMATO JELLY

MAKES:
1.3 kg/
3 lb

PREP TIME:
10–15 minutes,
plus straining
and cooling

COOKING TIME:
1–1 hour
20 minutes

900 g/2 lb firm, ripe tomatoes, rinsed and chopped

1 large orange (preferably unwaxed), scrubbed

2 lemon grass stalks, roughly chopped

5-cm/2-inch piece fresh ginger, peeled and chopped

1–2 whole star anise

3 whole cloves

900 ml/1½ pints water

3 tbsp white wine vinegar

about 900 g/2 lb preserving sugar (see method)

2 tbsp tomato purée

2 ripe tomatoes, deseeded and chopped

1. Place the tomatoes in a preserving pan. Roughly chop the orange and add to the pan. Lightly bruise the lemongrass and add to the pan with the ginger, star anise, whole cloves, water and vinegar. Place over a gentle heat, cover and simmer for 40–50 minutes, or until the tomatoes are soft. Leave to cool slightly before straining through a jelly bag.

2. Once all the juice has been extracted, measure and return to the rinsed-out preserving pan. Add the sugar, allowing 450 g/1 lb sugar for every 600 ml/1 pint juice. Heat gently, stirring frequently, until the sugar has completely dissolved, then stir in the tomato purée. Bring to the boil and boil rapidly for 10–20 minutes, or until setting point is reached.

3. Remove from the heat and leave to cool for 5–10 minutes, then skim before stirring in the 2 deseeded chopped tomatoes. Ladle into sterilized jars and cover the tops with waxed discs. Seal with non-metallic lids while hot, then leave to cool before labelling. Store in a cool, dark place. Once opened, store in the refrigerator.

GRAPE JELLY

MAKES:
900 g/2 lb

PREP TIME:
5–10 minutes,
plus straining
and cooling

COOKING TIME:
30–40 minutes

1 kg/2 lb 4 oz black grapes

about 450 g/1 lb granulated sugar (see method)

juice of 1 lemon

125 ml/4 fl oz fruit pectin extract

1. Strip the grapes from the stalks and put them into a large saucepan, cover and cook over a medium–low heat for 5 minutes, until the juices start to run. Mash well with a potato masher, then continue to cook, mashing 3–4 more times, for 15 minutes, until the fruit has disintegrated.

2. Remove the pan from the heat and pour the grapes and liquid into a jelly strainer set over a bowl. Leave to drain overnight without squeezing the bag.

3. Measure the juice and pour it into a preserving pan. Add 450 g/1 lb sugar for every 600 ml/1 pint juice and stir in the lemon juice and fruit pectin extract.

4. Set over a low heat and stir constantly until the sugar has dissolved. Increase the heat to high, bring to the boil and continue to boil for 20 minutes, or until setting point is reached. Remove from the heat and leave to cool for 5 minutes, then ladle into sterilized jars and cover the tops with waxed discs. Seal with lids while hot, then leave to cool before labelling. Store in a cool, dark place. Once opened, store in the refrigerator.

RED WINE JELLY

MAKES:
675 g/
1 lb 8 oz

PREP TIME:
5–10 minutes,
plus straining
and cooling

COOKING TIME:
45–50 minutes

450 g/1 lb Bramley apples

600 ml/1 pint water

1 bottle red wine,
such as claret

about 675 g/1 lb 8 oz
preserving sugar (see method)

1. Wash, core and chop the apples, then place them in a preserving pan together with the water and wine. Bring to the boil, then reduce the heat and simmer for 30 minutes, or until the apples are soft.

2. Strain the mixture through a jelly bag. Once all the juice has been extracted, measure and return to the rinsed-out preserving pan. Add the sugar, allowing 450 g/1 lb sugar for every 600 ml/1 pint juice. Heat gently, stirring frequently, until the sugar has dissolved. Bring to the boil and boil rapidly for 15 minutes, or until setting point is reached.

3. Remove from the heat and leave to cool for 5–10 minutes, then ladle into sterilized jars and cover the tops with waxed discs. Seal with non-metallic lids while hot, then leave to cool before labelling. Store in a cool, dark place. Once opened, store in the refrigerator.

Cook's tip: This recipe is delicious when made with mulled wine and is a wonderful winter-warmer gift. Simply infuse the red wine with spices, such as cinnamon, cloves and star anise, before adding to the apples and water in the pan.

TRADITIONAL CHUNKY MARMALADE

MAKES:
4.5 kg/
10 lb

PREP TIME:
10–15 minutes,
plus cooling

COOKING TIME:
1½–1¾ hours

1.5 kg/3 lb 5 oz Seville oranges (preferably unwaxed), scrubbed

juice of 2 large lemons

3.4 litres/6 pints water

2.7 kg/6 lb preserving sugar

1. Cut the oranges in half, squeeze out all the juice and reserve. Reserve all the pips from the oranges and tie in a small piece of muslin. Slice the peel into small chunks or strips and place in a preserving pan together with the orange and lemon juice and water. Add the bag of pips.

2. Simmer gently for 1½ hours, or until the peel is very soft and the liquid has reduced by half. Remove the bag of pips, carefully squeezing any juice into the pan. Add the sugar and heat, stirring, until the sugar has dissolved. Bring to the boil and boil rapidly for about 15 minutes, or until setting point is reached.

3. Remove from the heat and leave to cool for 5–10 minutes, then ladle into sterilized jars and cover the tops with waxed discs. Seal with lids while hot, then leave to cool before labelling. Store in a cool, dark place. Once opened, store in the refrigerator.

GINGER CITRUS MARMALADE

MAKES:
1.3 kg/
3 lb

PREP TIME:
10–15 minutes,
plus cooling

COOKING TIME:
1½–1¾ hours

4 limes (preferably unwaxed), scrubbed

2 large lemons (preferably unwaxed), scrubbed

2.5-cm/1-inch piece fresh ginger, peeled and chopped

1.2 litres/2 pints water

2 tsp ground ginger

about 900 g/2 lb preserving sugar (see method)

115 g/4 oz stem ginger, chopped

1. Cut off and discard both ends from the limes and lemons and wash the fruits thoroughly. Place in a large saucepan together with the chopped fresh ginger and the water. Bring to the boil then reduce the heat, cover and simmer for 1½ hours, or until the fruits are soft.

2. Cool slightly, then drain off the liquid and reserve. Chop the fruits as finely as possible, discarding the pips. Return the chopped fruits to the rinsed-out saucepan or a preserving pan, together with the reserved liquid and the ground ginger. Add the sugar, allowing 450 g/1 lb sugar for every 600 ml/1 pint liquid. Heat gently, stirring frequently, until the sugar has completely dissolved. Bring to the boil and boil rapidly for about 15 minutes, or until setting point is reached.

3. Remove from the heat and leave to cool for 5 minutes, then stir in the stem ginger. Ladle into sterilized jars and cover the tops with waxed discs. Seal with lids while hot, then leave to cool before labelling. Store in a cool, dark place. Once opened, store in the refrigerator.

REDUCED SUGAR MARMALADE

MAKES:
2.25 kg/
5 lb

PREP TIME:
15–20 minutes,
plus cooling

COOKING TIME:
1½–1¾ hours

1.5 kg/3 lb 5 oz oranges (preferably unwaxed), scrubbed

450 g/1 lb mandarin oranges (preferably unwaxed), scrubbed

1.7 litres/3 pints water

1.25 kg/2 lb 12 oz preserving sugar

1. Using a vegetable peeler, remove the peel as thinly as possible from 675 g/1 lb 8 oz of the oranges and 225 g/8 oz of the mandarins, then cut the peel into fine shreds. Place the peel in a small saucepan, cover with water and simmer for 30 minutes, or until soft. Drain and reserve.

2. Peel the remaining oranges and mandarins and cut all the fruits in half, discarding the bitter white pith from them. Reserve the pips and peel and tie up in a piece of muslin. Cut the fruit flesh into chunks and place in a large saucepan together with the water and the bag of pips and peel.

3. Bring to the boil, then reduce the heat, cover and simmer gently for 1 hour, or until the fruits are soft. Remove the muslin bag and discard. Transfer the mixture to a preserving pan. Add the sugar and heat gently, stirring frequently, until the sugar has completely dissolved. Bring to the boil and boil rapidly for 15 minutes, or until setting point is reached.

4. Remove from the heat and leave to cool for 5–8 minutes, then stir in the reserved shredded peel. Ladle into sterilized jars and cover the tops with waxed discs. Seal with lids while hot, then leave to cool before labelling. Store in a cool, dark place. Once opened, store in the refrigerator.

SPICY SQUASH MARMALADE

 **MAKES:**
2.25 kg/
5 lb

 PREP TIME:
10–15 minutes,
plus cooling

COOKING TIME:
1¼–1½ hours

900 g/2 lb butternut squash, peeled and deseeded, cut into small chunks

6 blood oranges (preferably unwaxed), scrubbed

150 ml/5 fl oz freshly squeezed lemon juice

2.5-cm/1-inch piece fresh ginger, peeled and grated

2 serrano chillies, deseeded and finely sliced

1.2 litres/2 pints water

1.25 kg/2 lb 12 oz preserving sugar

1. Place the squash in a large saucepan with a tight-fitting lid. Thinly slice two of the oranges without peeling, reserving the pips, and add to the saucepan. Peel the remaining oranges, chop the flesh and add to the pan together with the lemon juice, grated ginger and sliced chillies. Tie the orange pips in a piece of muslin and add to the pan with the water.

2. Bring to the boil, then reduce the heat, cover and simmer gently for 1 hour, or until the squash and oranges are soft. If preferred, transfer the mixture to a preserving pan.

3. Add the sugar and heat gently, stirring, until the sugar has dissolved. Bring to the boil and boil rapidly for 15 minutes, or until setting point is reached.

4. Remove from the heat and leave to cool for 10 minutes, skimming if necessary. Ladle into sterilized jars and cover the tops with waxed discs. Seal with lids while hot, then leave to cool before labelling. Store in a cool, dark place. Once opened, store in the refrigerator.

SAGE & ONION MARMALADE

MAKES:
900 g/2 lb

PREP TIME:
5–10 minutes,
plus cooling

COOKING TIME:
45–55 minutes

40 g/1½ oz butter

675 g/1 lb 8 oz red onions, sliced

4 tbsp granulated sugar

350 ml/12 fl oz pear cider

35 sage leaves, cut into narrow strips

½ tsp salt

1. Melt the butter in a saucepan, add the onions and sugar and cook over a medium heat, stirring occasionally, for 15–20 minutes, until very soft.

2. Add the pear cider, sage and salt, stir well and bring to the boil. Reduce the heat and simmer for 25–30 minutes, or until setting point is reached.

3. Remove from the heat and leave to cool for 8–10 minutes, then ladle into sterilized jars and cover the tops with waxed discs. Seal with lids while hot, then leave to cool before labelling. Store in a cool, dark place. Once opened, store in the refrigerator.

RED ONION MARMALADE

MAKES:
650 g/
1 lb 7 oz

PREP TIME:
20–25 minutes,
plus cooling

COOKING TIME:
1–1¼ hours

4 tbsp olive oil

900 g/2 lb red onions,
thinly sliced

85 g/3 oz demerara sugar

2 apples

6 tbsp red wine vinegar

1. Heat the oil in a large saucepan, add the onions, stir in the sugar and cook over a medium heat, stirring occasionally, for 40 minutes, until soft.

2. Peel, core and grate the apples, then add them to the pan with the vinegar. Simmer for 25 minutes, or until setting point is reached.

3. Remove the pan from the heat and leave to cool for 5 minutes, then ladle the marmalade into sterilized jars and cover the tops with waxed discs. Seal with non-metallic lids while hot, then leave to cool before labelling. Store in a cool, dark place. Once opened, store in the refrigerator.

CHILLI & GINGER MARMALADE

MAKES:
1.8 kg/4 lb

PREP TIME:
5–10 minutes,
plus cooling

COOKING TIME:
1½–1¾ hours

1 kg/2 lb 4 oz oranges (preferably unwaxed), scrubbed

3 x 8-cm/3¼-inch pieces fresh ginger, coarsely chopped

2 litres/3½ pints water, plus extra to make up volume (see method)

1.5 kg/3 lb 5 oz granulated sugar

4–5 fresh red chillies, deseeded and thinly sliced

1. Put the oranges and ginger into a preserving pan or other large saucepan, pour in the water and bring to the boil. Reduce the heat, cover and simmer for 1 hour.

2. Remove the oranges from the pan and leave to cool slightly. Strain the liquid into a bowl, reserving the ginger. Measure the liquid and return it to the pan. Add enough water to make it up to 1.5 litres/2¾ pints and then stir in the sugar.

3. Halve the oranges and scrape the pith, flesh and pips into a bowl. Finely shred the orange peel and ginger and add to the pan with the sliced chillies. Tie the pith, flesh and pips in a piece of muslin and add to the pan.

4. Bring to the boil over a medium heat and simmer for 20 minutes. Remove and discard the muslin bag and continue to simmer for a further 10–15 minutes, or until setting point is reached.

5. Remove from the heat and leave to cool for 8–10 minutes, then ladle into sterilized jars and cover the tops with waxed discs. Seal with lids while hot, then leave to cool before labelling. Store in a cool, dark place. Once opened, store in the refrigerator.

CURDS, BUTTERS & CHEESES

TRADITIONAL LEMON CURD

MAKES:
675 g/
1 lb 8 oz

PREP TIME:
5–10 minutes,
plus cooling

COOKING TIME:
25–30 minutes

4 lemons (preferably unwaxed), scrubbed

4 eggs, beaten

115 g/4 oz unsalted butter, diced

450 g/1 lb granulated sugar

1. Finely grate the rind from the lemons and squeeze out all the juice. Place the rind and juice in a heatproof non-metallic bowl, stir in the eggs, then add the butter and sugar.

2. Set the bowl over a pan of gently simmering water and stir until the sugar has dissolved and the butter has melted. Continue to cook, stirring frequently, for about 30 minutes, or until setting point is reached.

3. Remove the pan from the heat, ladle into sterilized jars and cover the tops with waxed discs. Seal with non-metallic lids while hot, then leave to cool before labelling. Store in the refrigerator. Use within 3 months.

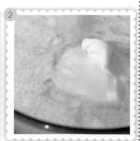

LIME CURD

MAKES:
650 g/
1 lb 7 oz

PREP TIME:
20–25 minutes,
plus cooling

COOKING TIME:
20–30 minutes

finely grated rind and juice of 10 limes

4 large eggs, lightly beaten

100 g/3½ oz unsalted butter, diced

225 g/8 oz caster sugar

2 tbsp set honey

1. Put all the ingredients into a large heatproof non-metallic bowl. Set the bowl over a pan of gently simmering water and stir until the sugar and honey have dissolved and the butter has melted.

2. Continue to cook, stirring constantly, for 20–30 minutes, or until setting point is reached.

3. Remove the pan from the heat, ladle into sterilized jars and cover the tops with waxed discs. Seal with non-metallic lids while hot, then leave to cool before labelling. Store in the refrigerator. Use within 4 weeks.

APPLE & ORANGE CURD

MAKES:
675 g/
1 lb 8 oz

PREP TIME:
15–20 minutes,
plus cooling
and straining

COOKING TIME:
35–40 minutes

450 g/1 lb Bramley apples, peeled, cored and chopped

150 ml/5 fl oz water

2 large oranges (preferably unwaxed), scrubbed

2 eggs, beaten

115 g/4 oz unsalted butter, diced

115 g/4 oz caster sugar

3–4 whole cloves

1. Place the apples and water in a large saucepan and cook for 10–12 minutes, or until soft. Remove from the heat and beat until smooth, then rub through a sieve into a heatproof non-metallic bowl.

2. Finely grate the rind from one of the oranges and squeeze out the juice from both oranges to give 150 ml/5 fl oz juice. Add to the bowl together with the eggs, butter, sugar and cloves. Set the bowl over a pan of gently simmering water and stir until the sugar has dissolved and the butter has melted.

3. Continue to cook, stirring frequently, for 20–30 minutes, or until setting point is reached.

4. Remove the pan from the heat and remove and discard the cloves. Ladle into sterilized jars and cover the tops with waxed discs. Seal with non-metallic lids while hot, then leave to cool before labelling. Store in the refrigerator. Use within 1 month.

Cook's tip: Use a cinnamon stick or two whole star anise in place of the cloves, adding them to the pan before heating the mixture, and removing (or straining) prior to potting.

GOOSEBERRY CURD

MAKES:
900 g/
2 lb

PREP TIME:
5–10 minutes,
plus straining
and cooling

COOKING TIME:
45–55 minutes

900 g/2 lb gooseberries, trimmed

3 tbsp water

55 g/2 oz butter

3 eggs, lightly beaten

450 g/1 lb granulated sugar

1. Put the gooseberries into a saucepan, add the water and bring to the boil over a medium heat. Reduce the heat, cover and simmer for 20–25 minutes, or until the gooseberries are soft.

2. Remove the pan from the heat and tip the contents into a nylon strainer set over a bowl, then rub the fruit through the sieve with the back of a ladle.

3. Set a heatproof bowl over a pan of gently simmering water, add the butter and leave it to melt, then stir in the gooseberry purée, eggs and sugar. Stir until the sugar has dissolved. Continue to cook, stirring frequently, for 20–30 minutes, or until setting point is reached.

4. Remove the pan from the heat, ladle into sterilized jars and cover the tops with waxed discs. Seal with non-metallic lids while hot, then leave to cool before labelling. Store in the refrigerator. Use within 3 weeks.

APRICOT CURD

MAKES:
1.8 kg/4 lb

PREP TIME:
5–10 minutes, plus straining and cooling

COOKING TIME:
50–55 minutes

675 g/1 lb 8 oz apricots

400 ml/14 fl oz water

115 g/4 oz unsalted butter, diced

juice of 2 lemons

4 eggs, lightly beaten

450 g/1 lb granulated sugar

1. Put the apricots into a saucepan, pour in the water and bring to the boil over a medium heat. Reduce the heat, cover and cook, stirring occasionally, for 15 minutes, or until the apricots are soft.

2. Remove the pan from the heat and tip the contents into a sieve set over a bowl. Rub the fruit through the sieve with the back of a spoon.

3. Melt the butter in a large heatproof non-metallic bowl set over a pan of gently simmering water, then stir in the apricot purée, lemon juice, eggs and sugar. Cook, stirring frequently, for 30–40 minutes, or until setting point is reached.

4. Remove the pan from the heat, ladle into sterilized jars and cover the tops with waxed discs. Seal with non-metallic lids while hot, then leave to cool before labelling. Store in the refrigerator. Use within 3 weeks.

PASSION FRUIT CURD

MAKES:
300 g/
10½ oz

PREP TIME:
10–15 minutes,
plus straining
and cooling

COOKING TIME:
20–25 minutes

3 large eggs

6 passion fruit, halved

115 g/4 oz unsalted butter, diced

115 g/4 oz granulated sugar

1 tbsp lemon juice

1. Lightly beat the eggs in a heatproof bowl. Scrape the passion fruit flesh into a non-stick pan. Add the butter and sugar to the pan and stir over a low heat, until the sugar has dissolved and the butter has melted, then bring to the boil. Remove the pan from the heat and whisk the mixture into the eggs until thoroughly combined.

2. Set the bowl over a pan of gently simmering water and cook, stirring frequently, for 15–20 minutes, or until setting point is reached.

3. Remove the pan from the heat and leave to cool completely, stirring occasionally. Strain the curd into a jug, pressing and rubbing the seeds with the back of a spoon to extract as much curd as possible. Stir in a few passion fruit seeds, if liked, and the lemon juice. Ladle into sterilized jars and cover the tops with waxed discs. Seal with non-metallic lids while hot, then leave to cool before labelling. Store in the refrigerator. Use within 2 weeks.

CRANBERRY CHEESE

MAKES:
1.6 kg/
3 lb 8 oz

PREP TIME:
5–10 minutes,
plus straining
and cooling

COOKING TIME:
1½–1¾ hours

1.3 kg/3 lb cranberries

850 ml/1½ pints water

1.3 kg/3 lb granulated sugar

2 tsp lemon juice

juice and finely grated rind of
½ orange

½ tsp ground cinnamon

1. Put the cranberries into a saucepan, pour in just enough of the water to cover and bring to the boil over a medium–high heat. Reduce the heat to low and simmer, occasionally squashing the berries with the back of a wooden spoon, for 15 minutes.

2. Remove the pan from the heat and tip the contents into a sieve set over a bowl. Rub the cranberries through the sieve with the back of a ladle.

3. Transfer the fruit purée to a preserving pan, add the sugar and stir over a low heat until the sugar has dissolved. Add the lemon juice, orange rind and juice and cinnamon, increase the heat and bring to the boil. Reduce the heat and simmer, stirring occasionally, for 1¼ hours, or until setting point is reached.

4. Remove from the heat, ladle into sterilized jars or ramekins and cover the tops with waxed discs. Seal with non-metallic lids while hot, then leave to cool before labelling. Store in a cool, dark place. Turn out to serve.

DAMSON CHEESE

 MAKES:
1.8 kg/4 lb

 PREP TIME:
15–20 minutes,
plus straining
and cooling

 COOKING TIME:
1½–1¾ hours

1.3 kg/3 lb damsons, stoned
and halved

600 ml/1 pint water

about 900 g–1.3 kg/2–3 lb
granulated sugar (see method)

1. Put the damsons into a large saucepan, pour in the water, cover and bring to the boil over a high heat. Reduce the heat and simmer, stirring occasionally, for 30 minutes, or until the damsons are soft.

2. Remove the pan from the heat and tip the contents into a sieve set over a bowl. Rub the fruit through the strainer with the back of a ladle.

3. Measure the fruit purée and put it into a preserving pan. Add 500 g/1 lb 2 oz sugar for every 500 ml/18 fl oz purée and bring to the boil, stirring constantly until the sugar has dissolved. Reduce the heat and simmer, stirring occasionally, for 1 hour, or until setting point is reached.

4. Remove from the heat, ladle into sterilized jars or ramekins and cover the tops with waxed discs. Seal with lids while hot, then leave to cool before labelling. Store in a cool, dark place. Turn out to serve.

Cook's tip: Damsons have quite a tart flavour, which makes this recipe the perfect accompaniment for an after-dinner cheese board.

BLACKBERRY & APPLE CHEESE

MAKES:
1.8 kg/4 lb

PREP TIME:
10–15 minutes,
plus straining
and cooling

COOKING TIME:
1¼–1½ hours

1 kg/2 lb 4 oz blackberries

450 g/1 lb tart green apples, peeled, cored and diced

600 ml/1 pint water

about 1.3 kg/3 lb granulated sugar (see method)

1. Put the blackberries and apples into a large saucepan, pour in the water and bring to the boil over a medium heat. Reduce the heat and simmer for 30 minutes, or until the apples are soft.

2. Remove the pan from the heat and tip the contents into a sieve set over a bowl. Press the fruit purée through the sieve with the back of a ladle. Measure the quantity of fruit purée, then pour it into a preserving pan. Add 500 g/1 lb 2 oz sugar for every 500 ml/18 fl oz purée.

3. Set the pan over a low heat and stir until the sugar has dissolved then increase the heat and bring to the boil. Reduce the heat and simmer, stirring occasionally, for 50–60 minutes, or until setting point is reached.

4. Remove from the heat, ladle into sterilized jars or ramekins and cover the tops with waxed discs. Seal with lids while hot, then leave to cool before labelling. Store in a cool, dark place. Turn out to serve.

PEAR & BLUEBERRY CHEESE

MAKES:
675 g/1 lb 8 oz

PREP TIME:
50 minutes,
plus straining
and cooling

COOKING TIME:
1¼–1½ hours

1 kg/2 lb 4 oz blueberries

450 g/1 lb pears, peeled,
cored and diced

600 ml/1 pint water

about 675 kg/1 lb 8 oz
granulated sugar (see method)

1. Put the blueberries and pears into a large saucepan,
pour in the water and bring to the boil over a medium
heat. Reduce the heat and simmer for 1 hour, or until
the blueberries are soft.

2. Remove the pan from the heat and tip the contents
into a sieve set over a bowl. Press the pulp through the
sieve with the back of a ladle. Measure the quantity of
fruit purée, then pour it into a preserving pan. Add
500 g/1 lb 2 oz sugar for every 500 ml/18 fl oz purée.

3. Set the pan over a low heat and stir until the sugar
has dissolved, then increase the heat and bring to the
boil. Reduce the heat and simmer, stirring occasionally,
for 25–30 minutes, or until setting point is reached.

4. Remove from the heat, ladle into sterilized jars or
ramekins and cover the tops with waxed discs. Seal with
lids while hot, then leave to cool before labelling. Store
in a cool, dark place. Turn out to serve.

Cook's tip: Substitute blueberries for raspberries,
but do bear in mind that as they are a juicier fruit, the
raspberries will yield a greater weight of fruit purée and
as a result, you will need to add more sugar.

SPICY QUINCE BUTTER

MAKES:
1.3 kg/3 lb

PREP TIME:
5–10 minutes,
plus straining
and cooling

COOKING TIME:
1¼–1½ hours

1.8 kg/4 lb quinces, quartered

450 ml/16 fl oz cider

about 450 g/1 lb sugar (see method)

2 tsp ground cinnamon

1 tsp ground cloves

½ tsp ground allspice

grated rind and juice of 1 lemon

1. Put the quinces into a preserving pan, pour in the cider and bring to the boil over a high heat. Reduce the heat and simmer, stirring occasionally, for 50–60 minutes, until the fruit is soft.

2. Remove the pan from the heat and tip the contents into a sieve set over a bowl. Rub the quince through the sieve with the back of a ladle. Measure the fruit purée, return it to the preserving pan and add 225 g/ 8 oz sugar for every 500 ml/18 fl oz fruit purée. Stir in the spices, lemon rind and juice.

3. Set the pan over a low heat and stir until the sugar has dissolved, then increase the heat and bring to the boil. Boil rapidly for 25–30 minutes, or until setting point is reached.

4. Remove the pan from the heat, ladle into sterilized jars and cover the tops with waxed discs. Seal with lids while hot, then leave to cool before labelling. Store in a cool, dark place. Once opened, store in the refrigerator.

APPLE BUTTER

MAKES:
1 kg/2 lb 4 oz

PREP TIME:
10–15 minutes, plus straining and cooling

COOKING TIME:
55–60 minutes

1.5 kg/3 lb 5 oz Bramley apples, washed

1.2 litres/2 pints sweet cider or apple juice

150 ml/5 fl oz water

150 ml/5 fl oz lemon juice

2 cinnamon sticks, lightly bruised

2 tbsp grated lemon rind

about 450 g/1 lb granulated sugar (see method)

1. Chop the apples into small chunks, (do not peel or core) and place in a preserving pan together with the cider, water, lemon juice, cinnamon sticks and lemon rind. Bring to the boil, then reduce the heat and simmer gently for 30 minutes, stirring occasionally, until the apples are soft. Remove and discard the cinnamon sticks.

2. Remove the pan from the heat and tip the contents into a sieve set over a bowl. Rub the apple mixture through the sieve with the back of a ladle. Measure the fruit purée, return it to the preserving pan and add 350 g/12 oz sugar for every 600 ml/1 pint apple purée.

3. Set the pan over a low heat and stir until the sugar has dissolved. Continue to cook, for 25–30 minutes, or until setting point is reached.

4. Remove the pan from the heat, ladle into sterilized jars and cover the tops with waxed discs. Seal with lids while hot, then leave to cool before labelling. Store in a cool, dark place. Once opened, store in the refrigerator.

PLUM BUTTER

MAKES:
675 g/
1 lb 8 oz

PREP TIME:
10–15 minutes,
plus straining
and cooling

COOKING TIME:
1–1¼ hours

1.5 kg/3 lb 5 oz ripe plums, washed, stoned and cut in half

600 ml/1 pint water

2 tbsp grated orange rind

300 ml/10 fl oz freshly squeezed orange juice

1½ tsp ground cinnamon

about 900 g/2 lb granulated sugar (see method)

1. Place the plums in a preserving pan with the water and bring to the boil. Reduce the heat and simmer gently for 40–50 minutes, or until the plums are soft. Remove the pan from the heat, leave to cool, then tip the contents into a sieve set over a bowl. Rub the plum mixture through the sieve with the back of a ladle. Measure the fruit purée and return it to the preserving pan.

2. Add the orange rind and juice with the cinnamon and heat gently for 10 minutes. Add the sugar, allowing 350 g/12 oz sugar to each 600 ml/1 pint purée and stir until the sugar has dissolved. Bring to the boil and boil for 10–15 minutes, or until setting point is reached.

3. Remove the pan from the heat, ladle into sterilized jars and cover the tops with waxed discs. Seal with non-metallic lids while hot, then leave to cool before labelling. Store in a cool, dark place. Use within 3 months and, once opened, store in the refrigerator.

Cook's tip: For super-smooth fruit butter, strain the fruit purée through a fine nylon sieve and push the mixture over the fabric with the back of a ladle or a wooden spoon – continue the process until the remainder in the sieve is almost dry, and repeat if necessary.

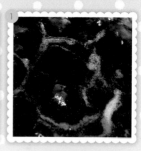

APRICOT & PASSION FRUIT BUTTER

 MAKES:
900 g/
2 lb

 PREP TIME:
10–15 minutes,
plus straining
and cooling

 COOKING TIME:
1–1¼ hours

675 g/1 lb 8 oz fresh apricots, washed and stoned

150 ml/5 fl oz freshly squeezed orange juice

600 ml/1 pint water, plus extra if needed

1 tsp ground allspice

3 ripe passion fruits

175–225 g/6–8 oz granulated sugar, or to taste

1. Place the apricots in a saucepan and add the orange juice and water. Bring to the boil, reduce the heat to a simmer, cover and cook for 45 minutes, or until the apricots are soft. If the liquid boils dry in this time, top up with more water, as necessary. Leave to cool, then rub through a sieve set over a bowl using a wooden spoon and transfer the purée to a preserving pan.

2. Add the ground allspice, the seeds and flesh from the passion fruits and 175 g/6 oz sugar. Heat gently, stirring, until the sugar has dissolved. Taste and add more sugar, if liked. Bring to the boil and boil for 10–15 minutes, until setting point is reached.

3. Remove the pan from the heat, ladle into sterilized jars and cover the tops with waxed discs. Seal with lids while hot, then leave to cool before labelling. Store in a cool, dark place. Once opened, store in the refrigerator.

CRUNCHY PEANUT BUTTER

MAKES:
175 g/6 oz

PREP TIME:
10 minutes

COOKING TIME:
No cooking

175 g/6 oz unsalted roasted peanuts

1 tbsp groundnut oil

1. Reserve 2 tablespoons of the peanuts. Mix together the remaining peanuts and oil and put the mixture into a food processor. Process until smooth, scraping down the sides of the bowl, if necessary.

2. Add the reserved peanuts and process for a further few seconds.

3. Transfer the peanut butter to an airtight container and store in the refrigerator for up to 2 weeks.

Cook's tip: To make smooth peanut butter, add all of the peanuts to the food processor in step 1, and process until smooth.

CHUTNEYS & PRESERVES

FRUITY APPLE CHUTNEY

 MAKES:
3.5 kg/
7 lb 11 oz

 PREP TIME:
15–20 minutes,
plus cooling

 COOKING TIME:
50 minutes–
1 hour

900 g/2 lb Bramley apples, peeled, cored and chopped

450 g/1 lb onions, chopped

450 g/1 lb ripe plums, rinsed, stoned and chopped

rind and juice of 2 lemons (preferably unwaxed), scrubbed

225 g/8 oz fresh cranberries

450 g/1 lb soft brown sugar

4 kiwi fruit, peeled and sliced

450 ml/16 fl oz malt vinegar

2 tbsp balsamic vinegar

1. Place the apples, onions and plums in a preserving pan with the lemon rind and juice and the cranberries. Cook over a gentle heat, stirring frequently, for 10 minutes, or until the cranberries are beginning to burst.

2. Stir in all the remaining ingredients and heat gently, stirring occasionally, until the sugar has dissolved. Bring to the boil, then reduce the heat and simmer for 35–40 minutes, or until setting point is reached.

3. Remove the pan from the heat and ladle into sterilized jars. Seal with non-metallic lids while hot, then leave to cool before labelling. Store in a cool, dark place for 4–6 weeks before using. Once opened, store in the refrigerator.

Cook's tip: If fresh cranberries aren't available, try frozen or dried instead. To plump dried cranberries, cover with hot water, soak for 20 minutes, then drain and add to the chutney as per the recipe instructions.

MANGO CHUTNEY

 MAKES:
1.3 kg/3 lb

 PREP TIME:
20–25 minutes,
plus standing
and cooling

 COOKING TIME:
1½–1¾ hours

1.7 litres/3 pints water

6 tbsp salt

1.3 kg/3 lb mangoes, peeled, halved, stoned and diced

600 ml/1 pint vinegar

450 g/1 lb granulated sugar

85 g/3 oz fresh ginger, peeled and finely chopped

10 garlic cloves, finely chopped

2 tsp crushed chillies

1 cinnamon stick

115 g/4 oz raisins

115 g/4 oz dried dates, stoned and chopped

1. Pour the water into a large bowl and stir in the salt until it has dissolved. Add the mangoes, cover with clingfilm and leave to stand for 24 hours.

2. Drain the diced mangoes. Pour the vinegar into a preserving pan or large saucepan, add the sugar and set over a low heat, stirring constantly, until the sugar has dissolved. Increase the heat to high and bring to the boil.

3. Add the mangoes, ginger, garlic, chillies, cinnamon, raisins and dates. Bring back to the boil, stirring occasionally, then reduce the heat and simmer, stirring occasionally, for 1¼–1½ hours, or until setting point is reached.

4. Remove the pan from the heat and ladle into sterilized jars. Seal with non-metallic lids while hot, then leave to cool before labelling. Store in a cool, dark place for 2–4 weeks before using. Once opened, store in the refrigerator.

SPICY TOMATO CHUTNEY

MAKES:
3.5 kg/
7 lb 10 oz

PREP TIME:
15–20 minutes,
plus cooling

COOKING TIME:
1–1¼ hours

1.5 kg/3 lb 5 oz firm ripe tomatoes, washed and chopped

450 g/1 lb Bramley apples, peeled, cored and chopped

450 g/1 lb red onions, chopped

1 head of celery, trimmed and chopped, leaves discarded

1 green jalapeño chilli, deseeded and chopped

675 g/1 lb 8 oz demerara sugar

1 tsp coriander seeds, lightly crushed

150 ml/5 fl oz water

600 ml/1 pint malt vinegar

4 tbsp balsamic vinegar

300 g/10½ oz sultanas

1. Place the tomatoes, apples, onions, celery, chilli and sugar in a preserving pan. Tie the coriander seeds in a small piece of muslin then add to the pan together with the water and cook over a gentle heat, stirring occasionally, for 30 minutes, or until the tomatoes and apples are soft.

2. Add both vinegars and the sultanas and bring to the boil, then reduce the heat and simmer for 35–45 minutes, or until setting point is reached.

3. Remove the pan from the heat and ladle into sterilized jars. Seal with non-metallic lids while hot, then leave to cool before labelling. Store in a cool, dark place for 2–4 weeks before using. Once opened, store in the refrigerator.

SWEET & SPICY TAMARIND CHUTNEY

MAKES:
250 g/9 oz

PREP TIME:
5–10 minutes, plus cooling

COOKING TIME:
35–40 minutes

100 g/3½ oz tamarind pulp, chopped

450 ml/16 fl oz water

½ fresh bird's eye chilli, or to taste, deseeded and chopped

55 g/2 oz soft light brown sugar, or to taste

½ tsp salt

1. Put the tamarind and water in a heavy-based saucepan over a high heat and bring to the boil. Reduce the heat to the lowest setting and simmer for 25 minutes, stirring occasionally to break up the tamarind pulp, or until tender.

2. Tip the tamarind pulp into a sieve and use a wooden spoon to push the pulp into the rinsed-out pan.

3. Stir in the chilli, sugar and salt and continue simmering for a further 10 minutes or until the desired consistency is reached. Leave to cool slightly, then stir in extra sugar or salt, to taste.

4. Leave to cool completely, then transfer to an airtight container and store in the refrigerator for up to 3 days before using. Once opened, store in the refrigerator.

SPICED PLUM CHUTNEY

MAKES:
1.8 kg/4 lb

PREP TIME:
20 minutes,
plus cooling

COOKING TIME:
1¼–1½ hours

1.2 litres/2 pints malt vinegar

900 g/2 lb granulated sugar

40 g/1½ oz salt

4 tbsp ground cinnamon

4 tbsp ground ginger

4 tbsp ground allspice

2.25 kg/5 lb plums, stoned and cut into quarters

1. Pour the vinegar into a preserving pan and add the sugar, salt and spices. Stir over a low heat until the sugar has dissolved, then increase the heat and bring to the boil.

2. Reduce the heat to low, add the plums and simmer, stirring occasionally, for about 1¼ hours, or until setting point is reached. Stir more frequently for the last 15 minutes of the cooking time.

3. Remove the pan from the heat and ladle into sterilized jars. Seal with non-metallic lids while hot, then leave to cool before labelling. Store in a cool, dark place for 4 weeks before using. Once opened, store in the refrigerator.

Cook's tip: Plum chutney is delicious with roast duck – remove the skins of the plums before cooking for a smoother texture that's perfect in crispy duck pancakes!

GREEN LEAF, OLIVE & PAPRIKA CHUTNEY

MAKES:
350 g/12 oz

PREP TIME:
5–10 minutes,
plus cooling

COOKING TIME:
20–25 minutes

225 g/8 oz fresh baby spinach leaves

handful of celery leaves

3 tbsp olive oil

2–3 garlic cloves, crushed

1 tsp cumin seeds

6–8 black olives, stoned and finely chopped

1 large bunch of fresh flat-leaf parsley leaves, finely chopped

1 large bunch of fresh coriander leaves, finely chopped

1 tsp smoked paprika

juice of ½ lemon

salt and pepper

toasted flatbread or crusty bread and black olives, to serve

1. Place the spinach and celery leaves in a steamer and steam until tender. Refresh the leaves under cold running water, drain well and squeeze out the excess water. Place the steamed leaves on a wooden chopping board and chop to a pulp.

2. Heat 2 tablespoons of the oil in a heavy-based casserole. Add the garlic and cumin seeds, then cook over a medium heat for 1–2 minutes, stirring, until they emit a nutty aroma. Stir in the olives with the parsley and coriander and add the paprika.

3. Toss in the pulped spinach and celery and cook over a low heat, stirring occasionally, for 10 minutes. Season with salt and pepper to taste.

4. Remove the pan from the heat and transfer the mixture to a bowl. Add the remaining oil and the lemon juice and mix well. When completely cold, transfer to an airtight container and store in the refrigerator. Use on the day of making.

SPICED PUMPKIN CHUTNEY

MAKES:
3.2 kg/7 lb

PREP TIME:
20–25 minutes,
plus cooling

COOKING TIME:
1 hour

1.3 kg/3 lb pumpkin, peeled, deseeded and coarsely chopped

1.3 kg/3 lb cooking apples, peeled, cored and coarsely chopped

450 g/1 lb onions, coarsely chopped

350 g/12 oz sultanas

850 ml/1½ pints white wine vinegar

2 tbsp ground ginger

1 tsp ground cloves

1 tsp pepper

1 tsp cayenne pepper

450 g/1 lb granulated sugar

1. Put the pumpkin, apples, onions and sultanas into a food processor and process until finely chopped, then transfer the mixture to a preserving pan or large saucepan. Add the vinegar, ginger, cloves, pepper and cayenne pepper and bring to the boil over a medium heat.

2. Reduce the heat and simmer, stirring occasionally, for 20 minutes, until slightly reduced. Stir in the sugar and cook, stirring until the sugar has completely dissolved. Increase the heat and continue cooking for about 30 minutes, or until setting point is reached.

3. Remove the pan from the heat and ladle into sterilized jars. Seal with non-metallic lids while hot, then leave to cool before labelling. Store in a cool, dark place for 4–6 weeks before using. Once opened, store in the refrigerator.

GOOSEBERRY & ELDERFLOWER CHUTNEY

MAKES:
1.1 kg/
2 lb 7 oz

PREP TIME:
15 minutes,
plus cooling

COOKING TIME:
1½–2 hours

1 kg/2 lb 4 oz gooseberries, trimmed

175 g/6 oz raisins

2 shallots, chopped

350 g/12 oz soft brown sugar

1½ tsp salt

1 tsp ground ginger

300 ml/10 fl oz white wine vinegar

10 elderflower teabags

1. Put the gooseberries, raisins, shallots, sugar, salt, ginger and vinegar into a preserving pan or large saucepan and bring to the boil over a low heat, stirring constantly until the sugar has dissolved.

2. Add the elderflower tea bags, increase the heat and bring to the boil. Reduce the heat and simmer, stirring occasionally, for 1¼–1½ hours, or until setting point is reached.

3. Remove the pan from the heat and remove and discard the elderflower teabags. Ladle into sterilized jars. Seal with non-metallic lids while hot, then leave to cool before labelling. Store in a cool, dark place for 4 weeks before using. Once opened, store in the refrigerator.

PEAR & GINGER CHUTNEY

MAKES:
1.8 kg/
4 lb

PREP TIME:
15–20 minutes,
plus standing
and cooling

COOKING TIME:
1½–1¾ hours

675 g/1 lb 8 oz pears, peeled, cored and coarsely chopped

3 onions, finely chopped

2 garlic cloves, finely chopped

1 cooking apple, cored and chopped

175 g/6 oz raisins

55 g/2 oz stem ginger, chopped

115 g/4 oz pecans or walnuts, chopped

grated rind and juice of 1 lemon

600 ml/1 pint cider vinegar

175 g/6 oz soft brown sugar

2 cloves

1 tsp salt

1. Put the pears, onions, garlic, apple, raisins, ginger, nuts, lemon juice and rind into a large non-metallic bowl.

2. Put the vinegar, sugar, cloves and salt into a saucepan and set over a low heat, stirring constantly, until the sugar has dissolved. Increase the heat and bring to the boil, then remove the pan from the heat and pour the mixture into the bowl with the pear mixture. Stir well, cover with clingfilm and leave to stand for 8–12 hours.

3. Tip the pear mixture into a preserving pan and bring to the boil over a high heat, stirring frequently. Reduce the heat and simmer, stirring occasionally, for 1¼–1½ hours, or until the fruit is soft and setting point is reached.

4. Remove the pan from the heat and ladle into sterilized jars. Seal with non-metallic lids while hot, then leave to cool before labelling. Store in a cool, dark place for 2–4 weeks before using. Once opened, store in the refrigerator.

SPICED CRANBERRY CHUTNEY

MAKES:
900 g/2 lb

PREP TIME:
20 minutes,
plus cooling

COOKING TIME:
15–20 minutes

1 orange

350 g/12 oz cranberries

1 large green apple, peeled, cored and diced

85 g/3 oz sultanas

25 g/1 oz shelled walnuts, chopped

350 g/12 oz granulated sugar

½ tsp ground cinnamon

½ tsp ground ginger

½ tsp ground allspice

3 tbsp orange juice

1 tbsp cider vinegar

1. Holding the orange over a bowl to catch the juice, cut off the rind, removing all traces of the bitter white pith. Cut between the membranes to remove the segments, then chop.

2. Put the chopped orange segments and any reserved orange juice into a preserving pan or large saucepan. Squeeze any remaining juice from the membranes into the pan, then discard the membranes. Add all the remaining ingredients and bring to the boil over a medium–high heat, stirring until the sugar has completely dissolved. Reduce the heat and simmer, stirring occasionally, for 15 minutes, or until all the cranberries have burst.

3. Remove the pan from the heat and leave to cool completely. Serve fresh on the day of making, or ladle into non-metallic airtight containers and store in the refrigerator for 2–3 days. Alternatively, freeze in the containers for up to 3 months.

Cook's tip: Tart, spicy chutney is the perfect antidote to the food excesses of Christmas and adds a delightful festive twist to cold meats, cheeses and crackers.

VANILLA & FIG PRESERVE

MAKES:
1.3 kg/3 lb

PREP TIME:
5–10 minutes,
plus cooling

COOKING TIME:
30–40 minutes

1½ lemons

900 g/2 lb figs, quartered

675 g/1 lb 8 oz granulated sugar

1 vanilla pod, split

4 tbsp Amaretto

1. Finely grate the rind and squeeze the juice from the lemons. Put the rind and juice into a preserving pan or large saucepan and add the figs and sugar. Scrape the seeds from the vanilla pod into the pan and add the pod.

2. Set the pan over a low heat and stir until the juices are beginning to run and the sugar has dissolved. Increase the heat and bring to the boil, stirring frequently.

3. Continue to boil, stirring constantly, for 15 minutes. Stir in the Amaretto and cook for 1 minute more.

4. Remove the pan from the heat, remove and discard the vanilla pod and leave to cool for 10–15 minutes. Ladle into sterilized jars and cover the tops with waxed discs. Seal with non-metallic lids while hot, then leave to cool before labelling. Store in a cool, dark place. Once opened, store in the refrigerator.

PEPPER POT PRESERVE

MAKES:
1.3 kg/3 lb

PREP TIME:
20–25 minutes,
plus cooling

COOKING TIME:
1–1¼ hours

450 g/1 lb Bramley apples, peeled, cored and chopped

450 g/1 lb onions, thinly sliced

3–4 garlic cloves, sliced

2–4 serrano chillies, deseeded and finely sliced

900 g/2 lb assorted coloured peppers, deseeded and finely chopped

450 g/1 lb demerara sugar, or add a little extra if a sweeter relish is preferred

1–3 tsp Tabasco sauce, or to taste

300 ml/10 fl oz red wine vinegar

85 ml/3 fl oz balsamic vinegar

1. Place the apples in a preserving pan together with the onions, garlic, chillies and peppers. Sprinkle with the sugar then add the Tabasco sauce. Simmer over a gentle heat for 15 minutes, stirring frequently, until the apples and onions are beginning to soften.

2. Add the vinegars and continue to simmer for 40 minutes, or until a thick consistency is reached and the liquid is absorbed. Check the sweetness and if necessary add a little extra sugar, then simmer for a further 10 minutes.

3. Remove from the heat and leave to cool for 5 minutes. Pot into warmed sterilized jars and cover the tops with waxed discs. Seal with non-metallic lids while hot, then leave to cool before labelling. Store in a cool, dark place. Once opened, store in the refrigerator.

Cook's tip: To transform this into a Roast Red Pepper Preserve, exchange the assorted coloured peppers for red peppers, and bake the chillies and peppers in a preheated oven at 220°C/425°F/Gas Mark 7, until the skins are blackened. Peel and then add to the pan with the apples and onions, and proceed as instructed.

SWEET BEETROOT PRESERVE

MAKES:
2.25 kg/5 lb

PREP TIME:
15–20 minutes,
plus cooling

COOKING TIME:
45–50 minutes

900 g/2 lb raw beetroot, peeled and grated or finely chopped

225 g/8 oz onions, finely chopped

450 g/1 lb Bramley apples, peeled, cored and finely chopped

grated rind and juice of 2 oranges (preferably unwaxed), scrubbed

850 ml/1½ pints malt vinegar

300 ml/10 fl oz water

450 g/1 lb demerara sugar

225 g/8 oz seedless raisins

1. Place the beetroot in a preserving pan with the onions, apples, orange rind and juice. Add the vinegar and water and bring to the boil. Reduce the heat and simmer for 15 minutes.

2. Add the sugar and heat gently, stirring frequently, until the sugar has completely dissolved, then stir in the raisins. Simmer for a further 30 minutes, or until the beetroot is soft.

3. Remove the pan from the heat, ladle into sterilized jars and cover the tops with waxed discs. Seal with non-metallic lids while hot, then leave to cool before labelling. Store in a cool, dark place. Once opened, store in the refrigerator.

Cook's tip: Raw beetroot will dye anything it comes into contact with, including skin, fabric and work surfaces – so wear gloves and an apron when preparing this preserve. If stains do transfer to your clothing, soak in warm water and wash with bio-detergent to remove the offending splodge!

RASPBERRY & APPLE PRESERVE

MAKES:
900 g/2 lb

PREP TIME:
5–10 minutes,
plus standing
and cooling

COOKING TIME:
4–5 minutes

600 g/1 lb 5 oz Bramley apples, peeled, cored and chopped

600 g/1 lb 5 oz fresh ripe raspberries, rinsed

225 ml/8 fl oz lemon juice

450 g/1 lb granulated sugar

225 ml/8 fl oz liquid pectin

1. Layer all the fruits with the lemon juice, sugar and pectin in a large non-metallic bowl. Cover with clingfilm and leave to stand overnight.

2. Pour the mixture into a preserving pan. Bring to the boil, stirring occasionally, and boil for 4 minutes. Remove from the heat and leave to cool for 5 minutes.

3. Ladle into warmed sterilized jars and cover the tops with waxed discs. Seal with non-metallic lids while hot, then leave to cool before labelling. Store in a cool, dark place. Once opened, store in the refrigerator and use within 10 days.

SUMMER BERRY PRESERVE

MAKES:
1.8 kg/4 lb

PREP TIME:
5–10 minutes,
plus cooling

COOKING TIME:
5–10 minutes

900 g/2 lb assorted berries,
such as blueberries,
cranberries, raspberries and
strawberries, hulled and rinsed

3 tbsp lemon juice

900 g/2 lb granulated sugar

1 tsp butter

225 ml/8 fl oz liquid pectin

1. Place all the fruits in a large preserving pan with the lemon juice and sugar. Heat gently, stirring occasionally, until the sugar has dissolved. Add the butter.

2. Bring to the boil and boil rapidly for 3 minutes, then remove from the heat and stir in the pectin. Leave to cool before skimming.

3. Ladle into warmed sterilized jars and cover the tops with waxed discs. Seal with non-metallic lids while hot, then leave to cool before labelling. Store in a cool, dark place. Once opened, store in the refrigerator.

Cook's tip: Use frozen mixed summer berries in place of fresh. Defrost overnight, then drain off any excess liquid and add to the pan with the lemon juice and sugar. Alternatively, use a single type of berry for a concentrated fruity flavour.

PICKLES & RELISHES

SWEETCORN RELISH

MAKES: 950 g/ 2 lb 2 oz

PREP TIME: 10–15 minutes, plus cooling

COOKING TIME: 20–25 minutes

3 corn cobs

1 red pepper

1 jalapeño chilli

125 ml/4 fl oz cider vinegar

100 g/3½ oz soft light brown sugar

1 tbsp salt

1 tbsp ground mustard seeds

½ tsp celery seeds

1 red onion, diced

1. Cut the kernels off the corn cobs. Deseed and dice the red pepper and the chilli.

2. Put the corn, red pepper, chilli, vinegar, sugar, salt, mustard seeds and celery seeds into a large saucepan over a medium–high heat and bring to the boil. Reduce the heat and simmer, stirring occasionally, for about 15 minutes until the mixture reduces slightly. The sugar will melt, producing enough liquid to cover the vegetables.

3. Stir the onion into the corn mixture, remove from the heat and ladle into sterilized jars. Seal with non-metallic lids while hot, then leave to cool before labelling. Store in the refrigerator. Use within 1 week.

DILL PICKLES

MAKES:
2.5 litres/
4½ pints

PREP TIME:
25 minutes,
plus cooling

COOKING TIME:
10–15 minutes

6 small cucumbers,
cut into 1-cm/½-inch slices,
or lengthways into quarters

6 bay leaves

3 tbsp dill seeds

3 garlic cloves, thinly sliced

1 litre/1¾ pints white wine
vinegar

450 ml/16 fl oz water

115 g/4 oz salt

1. Pack the cucumber into sterilized jars, putting the bay leaves, dill seeds and garlic slices in amongst the slices.

2. Pour the vinegar and water into a saucepan, add the salt and bring to the boil. As soon as the mixture reaches boiling point, remove the pan from the heat.

3. Pour the vinegar mixture into the jars. Seal with non-metallic lids while hot, then leave to cool before labelling. Store in a cool, dark place for 1 week before using. Once opened, store in the refrigerator.

MIXED VEGETABLE PICKLE

MAKES:
2.7 kg/
6 lb

PREP TIME:
15–20 minutes,
plus standing
and cooling

COOKING TIME:
30–40 minutes

2 kg/4 lb 8 oz mixed
vegetables, such as
cauliflower, carrots, baby
onions, celery and cucumber,
chopped into small pieces

6 garlic cloves, chopped

175 g/6 oz salt

1.2 litres/2 pints boiling water

225 g/8 oz granulated sugar

1 tbsp mustard powder

1 tbsp ground turmeric

1.2 litres/2 pints malt vinegar

5-cm/2-inch piece fresh
ginger, peeled and grated

3 tbsp plain flour

1. Place the vegetables and garlic in a large bowl. In
another bowl, dissolve the salt in the boiling water and
pour over the vegetables. Cover and leave to stand for
24 hours.

2. The next day, drain and rinse the vegetables. Drain
again and place in a preserving pan. Mix the sugar
with the mustard powder and turmeric, then mix in
half the vinegar. Pour over the vegetables, stir in the
grated ginger and bring to the boil. Reduce the heat
and simmer for 20 minutes, or until the vegetables are
just tender.

3. Blend the flour with the remaining vinegar and stir
into the vegetables. Cook, stirring, for 5 minutes, or until
the liquid thickens.

4. Remove from the heat and leave to cool for
5 minutes and then ladle into sterilized jars. Seal with
non-metallic lids while hot, then leave to cool before
labelling. Store in a cool, dark place. Once opened,
store in the refrigerator.

BREAD & BUTTER PICKLES

MAKES:
3 litres/
5¼ pints

PREP TIME:
15–20 minutes,
plus standing
and cooling

COOKING TIME:
15–20 minutes

1.8 kg/4 lb cucumbers,
thinly sliced

6 onions, thinly sliced

1 red pepper, deseeded and
chopped

1 green pepper, deseeded
and chopped

70 g/2½ oz sea salt

1 litre/1¾ pints cracked ice

950 g/2 lb 2 oz granulated
sugar

½ tsp ground cloves

1 tsp ground turmeric

1 tsp celery seeds

2 tbsp mustard seeds

1.2 litres/2 pints white wine
vinegar

1. Put the cucumbers, onions, peppers, salt and ice into a large non-metallic bowl and mix well. Transfer to a large colander, set over a bowl. Put a weighted plate on top of the vegetables and leave to drain in the refrigerator for 3 hours.

2. Mix together the sugar, spices and vinegar in a preserving pan, stirring until the sugar has dissolved. Drain the vegetables thoroughly, pressing out as much liquid as possible, then add to the pan. Bring to the boil over a medium heat, stirring occasionally.

3. Remove the pan from the heat and ladle the pickles into sterilized jars. Seal with non-metallic lids while hot, then leave to cool before labelling. Store in a cool, dark place for 4–6 weeks before using. Once opened, store in the refrigerator.

CHILLI PICKLED ONIONS

MAKES:
1.5 litres/
2¾ pints

PREP TIME:
15–20 minutes,
plus standing
and cooling

COOKING TIME:
10–15 minutes

1 kg/2 lb 4 oz pickling onions or shallots, peeled

55 g/2 oz salt

1 litre/1¾ pints white wine vinegar

1 tsp cloves

9 dried red chillies

6 small tarragon sprigs

1. Put the onions into a non-metallic bowl, sprinkle with the salt and shake the bowl well. Cover with clingfilm and leave to stand overnight. Uncover, rinse and pat dry, then spread out on a tea towel.

2. Pour the vinegar into a saucepan, add the cloves and bring to the boil over a medium heat. Reduce the heat and simmer for 10 minutes, then remove from the heat and leave to cool.

3. Pack the onions, chillies and tarragon into sterilized jars. Strain the vinegar into a jug, then pour into the jars to cover the onions. Seal with non-metallic lids while hot, then leave to cool before labelling. Store in a cool, dark place for 4–6 weeks before using. Once opened, store in the refrigerator.

PICKLED SHALLOTS IN BALSAMIC VINEGAR

MAKES:
2 litres/
3 ½ pints

PREP TIME:
15–20 minutes,
plus standing
and cooling

COOKING TIME:
15 minutes

1.2 litres/2 pints water

115 g/4 oz sea salt

900 g/2 lb shallots, peeled

300 ml/10 fl oz balsamic vinegar

600 ml/1 pint white wine vinegar

2 dried red chillies

2 mace blades

6 allspice berries, lightly crushed

6 black peppercorns

1 cinnamon stick

2 bay leaves

1. Pour the water into a large non-metallic bowl and stir in the salt until it has dissolved. Add the shallots, cover them with a weighted plate to keep them submerged, and leave to stand for 2 days.

2. Pour both types of vinegar into a large pan and add the chillies, mace, allspice berries, peppercorns, cinnamon stick and bay leaves. Bring to the boil over a low heat, then remove from the heat and leave to cool.

3. Drain the shallots and rinse under cold running water, then drain again and pat dry with kitchen paper. Pack the shallots into sterilized jars.

4. Strain the cooled vinegar into a jug, then pour it over the shallots to cover them completely. Seal with non-metallic lids, then leave to cool completely before labelling. Store in a cool, dark place for 4–6 weeks before using. Once opened, store in the refrigerator.

Cook's tip: To make light work of peeling lots of shallots, soak in boiling water for 2–3 minutes, then drain and rinse under cold water. When cool enough to handle, trim the top and bottom of each of the shallots and peel away the papery skin.

CHILLI PICKLED GARLIC

MAKES:
1 litre/
1¾ pints

PREP TIME:
30–40 minutes,
plus cooling

COOKING TIME:
10–15 minutes

500 ml/18 fl oz cider vinegar

5 tbsp water

1 tbsp salt

70 g/2½ oz sugar

1 tsp coriander seeds

1 tsp crushed chillies

150 garlic cloves
(12–13 bulbs), peeled

1. Pour the vinegar and the water into a large saucepan, add the salt and sugar and bring to the boil over a medium heat, stirring constantly until the salt and sugar have dissolved. Reduce the heat, add the coriander seeds and chillies and simmer for 5 minutes.

2. Add the garlic cloves, bring back to the boil and boil for 1 minute. Remove the pan from the heat and strain the mixture into a jug. Set aside the garlic cloves and spices.

3. Pack the garlic cloves and spices into sterilized jars, pour over the vinegar mixture and leave to cool. Seal with non-metallic lids while hot, then leave to cool completely before labelling. Store in a cool, dark place for 2–3 weeks before using. Once opened, store in the refrigerator.

PICKLED RED CABBAGE

MAKES:
2 litres/
3½ pints

PREP TIME:
10–15 minutes,
plus standing
and cooling

COOKING TIME:
15–20 minutes

1 kg/2 lb 4 oz red cabbage,
cored and shredded

55 g/2 oz salt

1.5 litres/2¾ pints red wine
vinegar

2 tsp ground coriander

1 tsp ground cinnamon

1 tsp ground allspice

½ tsp pepper

2 bay leaves, crumbled

1. Place the cabbage in a non-metallic bowl and sprinkle with the salt. Cover with clingfilm and leave to stand for 24 hours.

2. Pour the vinegar into a preserving pan or other large saucepan, stir in the spices and bay leaves and bring to the boil over a medium heat. Reduce the heat and simmer for 10 minutes, then remove the pan from the heat and leave to cool.

3. Rinse the cabbage under cold running water and pat dry with kitchen paper. Pack it into sterilized jars and strain the vinegar over, removing and discarding the spices and bay leaves. Seal with non-metallic lids while hot, then leave to cool completely before labelling. Store in a cool, dark place for 5 days before using. Consume within 3 weeks. Once opened, store in the refrigerator.

GARLIC & CHILLI PICCALILLI

MAKES:
1.6 kg/
3 lb 8 oz

PREP TIME:
20–25 minutes,
plus standing
and cooling

COOKING TIME:
15–20 minutes

350 g/12 oz cauliflower, broken into small florets

350 g/12 oz pickling onions or small shallots, halved

225 g/8 oz runner beans, de-stringed and cut into 2-cm/¾-inch pieces

225 g/8 oz courgettes or marrow, cut into 2-cm/¾-inch chunks

225 g/8 oz salt

1.7 litres/3 pints water

150 g/5½ oz golden caster sugar

850 ml/1½ pints distilled malt vinegar

4-cm/1½-inch piece fresh ginger, grated

5 garlic cloves, finely chopped

1 large mild red chilli, deseeded and finely chopped

1½ tbsp mustard seeds

1½ tbsp coriander seeds

4 tbsp cornflour

4 tsp ground turmeric

1 tbsp dry English mustard powder

1. Mix together the vegetables, salt and water in a large bowl. Cover and leave to stand for 24 hours.

2. Drain the vegetables, rinse well and drain again. Place them in a large saucepan with the sugar, 700 ml/1¼ pints of the vinegar, the ginger, garlic, chilli, mustard seeds and coriander seeds and bring to the boil. Simmer for 10–12 minutes until the vegetables are tender but still firm to the bite.

3. Blend the remaining vinegar with the cornflour, turmeric and mustard powder, then stir into the vegetables and simmer for 2–3 minutes until thickened.

4. Remove from the heat, ladle into sterilized jars and cover with non-metallic lids. When completely cool, label and store in a cool, dark place for 4–6 weeks before using. Once opened, store in the refrigerator.

SOUR PICKLES

MAKES:
5 litres/
8¾ pints

PREP TIME:
20 minutes,
plus cooling

COOKING TIME:
20 minutes

2 litres/3½ pints cider vinegar

85 g/3 oz rock salt

100 g/3½ oz granulated sugar

100 g/3½ oz mustard seeds

450 ml/16 fl oz water

24 kirby or baby cucumbers, sliced lengthways

1. Pour the vinegar into a saucepan, add the salt, sugar, mustard seeds and the water and bring to the boil.

2. Meanwhile, pack the cucumber slices into sterilized jars.

3. Remove the pan from the heat and pour the mixture into the jars, leaving a 1-cm/½-inch gap at the top of the jar. Cover with non-metallic lids and leave to cool, then label and store in a cool, dark place for 1 month before using. Once opened, store in the refrigerator.

LEMON & CHILLI RELISH

 MAKES:
250 ml/
9 fl oz

 PREP TIME:
15 minutes,
plus cooling

 COOKING TIME:
No cooking

3 lemons

1 orange

4 tbsp chopped coriander

3 tbsp clear honey

1 tbsp red wine vinegar

1–2 green chillies, deseeded
(optional) and chopped

salt

1. Cut the rind off the lemons, removing all traces of bitter white pith. Using a small, sharp knife, cut out the segments over a bowl to catch the juices. Remove and discard the membranes and seeds, chop the segments and put them into a non-metallic bowl. Repeat with the orange.

2. Add all the remaining ingredients and season with a pinch of salt. Mix well, cover with clingfilm and leave to stand in the refrigerator for 4 hours before serving. Serve immediately or ladle into a non-metallic airtight container and freeze for up to 1 month.

PICKLED JALAPENOS

MAKES:
950 g/
2 lb 2 oz

PREP TIME:
15 minutes,
plus cooling

COOKING TIME:
10–15 minutes

450 g/1 lb jalapeño chillies

1 white onion

8 garlic cloves

700 ml/1¼ pints cider vinegar or white distilled vinegar

2 tbsp salt

2 bay leaves

2 tsp sugar

1. Remove the stems from the jalapeños and cut the chillies into thick rings.

2. Peel and roughly chop the onion. Peel the garlic cloves.

3. Bring the vinegar, salt, bay leaves and sugar to the boil in a large saucepan. Add the chillies, onions and garlic. Reduce the heat and simmer for about 5 minutes, or until the chillies are tender.

4. Strain the vinegar mixture into a jug, removing and discarding the bay leaves, then ladle the chillies, onions and garlic into sterilized jars. Pour the vinegar into the jars to cover the chillies, then cover with non-metallic lids. When completely cool, label and store in the refrigerator for up to 2 months.

BLUEBERRY RELISH

MAKES:
1.3 kg/
3 lb

PREP TIME:
15–20 minutes,
plus cooling

COOKING TIME:
35–40 minutes

900 g/2 lb fresh blueberries, rinsed

2 large Bramley apples, peeled, cored and finely chopped

300 g/10½ oz onions, finely chopped

1 large red pepper, deseeded and finely chopped

2–3 fresh rosemary sprigs

225–350 g/8–12 oz light muscovado sugar, or to taste

300 ml/10 fl oz white wine vinegar

3 tbsp balsamic vinegar

1. Place the blueberries, apples, onions, red pepper and rosemary sprigs in a preserving pan. Stir in the sugar (add the minimum amount, then add more according to taste later) with the white wine vinegar. Bring to the boil, then reduce the heat, cover and simmer for 30 minutes, or until the fruit is soft and the liquid thickened. Add a little water if the liquid has evaporated and reduce the heat, if necessary.

2. Remove and discard the rosemary sprigs and stir in the balsamic vinegar. Cook for a further 5 minutes.

3. Remove the pan from the heat and leave to cool for 5–10 minutes, then ladle into sterilized jars. Cover with non-metallic lids, when completely cool, label and store in a cool, dark place. Once opened, store in the refrigerator.

TOMATO & RED ONION RELISH

MAKES:
350 ml/
12 fl oz

PREP TIME:
15 minutes,
plus cooling

COOKING TIME:
1½–1¾ hours

8 ripe tomatoes

1 tbsp virgin olive oil, plus extra for drizzling

2 large red onions, thinly sliced

55 g/2 oz rocket or baby spinach leaves

salt and pepper

1. Preheat the oven to 150°C/300°F/Gas Mark 2. Cut the tomatoes in half and arrange all the halves on a large roasting tray. Drizzle with oil and season to taste with salt and pepper. Cook in the oven for 1¼–1½ hours, or until roasted but still moist. Set aside to cool.

2. Heat the oil in a large frying pan. Add the onions and fry over a gentle heat until soft and golden brown. Place eight of the oven-dried tomato halves in a food processor or blender and process until puréed. Add to the onions in the frying pan.

3. Slice the remaining eight tomato halves and add to the frying pan with the rocket. Season to taste with salt and pepper and cook until the leaves have just wilted. Serve immediately.